CW00518386

Diamond Ju| Songbook

Music of Pageantry & Patriotism arranged for piano, voice & guitar.

Published by
Wise Publications
14-15 Berners Street, London, W1T 3LJ, UK.

Exclusive distributors:
Music Sales Limited
Distribution Centre, Newmarket Road, Bury St Edmunds, Suffolk, IP33 3YB, UK.
Music Sales Pty Limited
20 Resolution Drive, Caringbah, NSW 2229, Australia.

Order No. AM1005543
ISBN 978-1-78038-733-8

This book was previously sold as Rule Britannia! AM986106

Preface by Graham Vickers.
Music processed by Paul Ewers Music Design.
Cover photograph courtesy of Getty Images.
Cover background image courtesy of Fotolia.

Printed in the EU.

www.musicsales.com

WISE PUBLICATIONS
part of The Music Sales Group

London / New York / Paris / Sydney / Copenhagen / Berlin / Madrid / Hong Kong / Tokyo

Part II:
Traditional Favourites

Part III:
Patriotic Tributes

Music, Patriotism and the British Monarchy

Brit13sh Royalty's relationship with music has been an enduring if uneven one for many centuries. Although the mood created by the stirring anthems that accompany great royal occasions is invariably one of continuity and permanence, this effect has sometimes been generated more by the evocative power of the compositions themselves than by natural empathy between musicians and monarchs.

Music in particular and the arts in general have not always been held in high esteem by British kings and queens. George II apparently 'hated all poets and painters' and George V, whose main passion seems to have been stamp collecting, wanted nothing other than *Land of Hope and Glory* played at the opening of the British Empire Exhibition (and it remains questionable whether he even wanted that).

On the other hand, Frederick, Prince of Wales (1707-1751), who died before he was able to become monarch, played the cello, and some two hundred years earlier Henry VIII had maintained a virtual supergroup of court musicians comprising '15 trumpets, 3 lutes, 3 rebecks, 3 tamborets, a harp, 2 viols, 9 sackbuts, a fife and four drumslades.'

Predating music-loving Henry was Edward IV, who reigned from 1461 to 1483 (with a break of a few months in the period 1470–1471) and who is recorded as having employed thirteen minstrels, 'whereof some be trumpets, some with shalmes and small pypes.' Henry himself was an amateur musician, and is tentatively credited with composing the melody for *Greensleeves*.

In the fifteenth century the Sovereign's growing house band was finally given a formal title, 'The Musick', but not until the reign of Charles I was the post of Master of the King's Musick created. Lutenist Nicholas Lanier was the first appointee, taking up office in 1626. He was to provide music for a variety of court entertainments, including the 1617 masque *Lovers Made Men*, the first appearance in England of this now lost Italian-style recitativo.

This formal recognition of the function of 'musick' in royal life was initially followed by an optimistic expansion of its activities—during the reign of James II in the late seventeenth century the Musick and its Master were given several additional commemorative duties to perform.

These duties took the form of the composition (by The Master) of odes to celebrate royal occasions such as the King's birthday, and these odes were then performed by the Musick and members of The Chapel Royal. What had previously been a form of court entertainment was now being tentatively pressed into service to help commemorate—and eventually to project—the image of royalty.

Henry VIII playing the harp ('Psalter of Henry VIII' by Jean Mallard, © The British Library)

Portrait of Henry Purcell

There was no more willing accomplice in this type of musical celebration of the monarch than the musical prodigy Henry Purcell, whose earliest composition—written in 1670 when he was eleven years old—took the form of an ode to King Charles II's birthday. Twenty-five years later his anthem and two elegies (including *Thou Knowest Lord*) would be played at the funeral of Queen Mary II.

In another of those intermittent blips that seem to characterise the relationship between sovereign and music at court, the expanded duties given to The Musick were for some reason suspended and the Master's official duties were gradually downgraded to the attendance of royal weddings, baptisms and suchlike.

It seemed as if the royal role of music was set to diminish or disappear. The next major development in the relationship between music and the monarch would, however, be both vibrant and influential.

Queen Anne's reign (1702-1714) saw the emergence of George Frideric Handel, the composer whose fortunes were to be forever closely associated with British royalty. His musical career began in his native Germany where, in 1710, he became Kapellmeister to George, Elector of Hanover, the man who was later to become George I of Great Britain. Handel visited Britain (absenting himself without official leave from his duties in Hanover for two years) and then settled permanently in London, where he received a yearly income of £200 from Queen Anne.

Upon Anne's death, George I arrived in England to take up the throne (the consequence of a deal brokered to exclude Catholics from the British throne by designating George's mother, Electress Sophie, as the closest Protestant relative of the British Royal Family) and his old relationship with Handel was cautiously revived.

Initially relations were frosty because Handel's unofficial leave of absence from his post at Kapellmeister still rankled, however legend has it that the composer restored himself to the good favour of Britain's first Hanoverian monarch with a composition to be played as a surprise for a royal boating party. This was subsequently published in 1740 under the title *Water Music*.

Handel was made official court composer in 1723 and he wrote a number of operas (including *Giulio Cesare*) in that busy year. In 1726 his opera *Scipio* was performed for the first time and its march was to become and remain the regimental slow march of the British Grenadier Guards.

'Ball At St. James's Palace on Her Majesty's Birth Night' after Daniel Dodd, circa 1781 (The Royal Collection © 2005, Her Majesty Queen Elizabeth II)

In the following year George I died and Handel was commissioned to compose four pieces for the coronation of his son and successor King George II. The composer chose various texts from the King James Bible that were traditionally used in the coronation ceremony, now setting them to music and scoring them for orchestra and a four-part choir.

The result was to provide one of the most potent and enduring demonstrations of the power of music to inhabit and promote the image of British royalty.

Although composed specifically for George II's coronation—and utilising texts that were already customarily used on such occasions—Handel's works included one that has been sung at every single British coronation since that of George II. *Zadok the Priest*, which describes the anointing of King Solomon, it is a powerful piece of cultural propaganda that links biblical anointing rites with those performed in the British coronation ceremony.

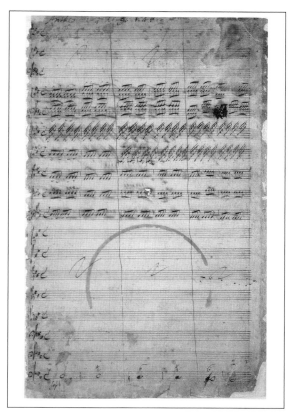

Beginning of 'Zadok The Priest' by George Frideric Handel (© The British Library)

The textual connection was already there but Handel's music gave emotional reinforcement to the idea of the British monarch enjoying not just secular privilege but divine connections.

*Zadok the Priest and Nathan the Prophet
anointed Solomon King.
And all the people rejoic'd, and said:
God save the King, long live the King,
may the King live for ever!
Amen, Alleluia!*

Despite this triumphant welcoming of a new king, the Hanoverian dynasty, which was to rule Britain until 1901, was not always known for its love of the arts. As has already been noted, George II railed against all poets and painters although he did retain some fondness for music. The troubled George III, who famously descended into madness, was in fact particularly fond of Handel's music.

The roles of both the Musick and the Master gradually diminished up to and throughout the reign of Queen Victoria so that by the time of the 1901 coronation of

George Frideric Handel, court composer to King George I and King George II

her successor Edward VII (whose marriage to Alexandra of Denmark had already been commemorated by the composition of *God Bless The Prince Of Wales*), the band no longer performed any concerts at all and was reduced to playing sporadically at court functions.

Eventually, under George V, who reigned 1910-1936, the number of musicians with Court appointments dwindled to such an extent that the title Master of the King's Musick became a purely honorary one. That it was not abolished altogether was largely due to the efforts of Sir Edward Elgar, who served in the role from 1924 to 1934 after bitterly complaining to the king's secretary that to ditch the position altogether would be for Britain to lose the 'last shred of connexion of the Court to Art.'

The archaic spelling of 'musick' was dropped at the time of Elgar's tenure, during which he put the royal collection of musical instruments in good order and composed *The Nursery Suite,* which was dedicated to the child princesses Elizabeth and Margaret. Among

Sir Edward Elgar, Master of the King's Music from 1924-1934

his other works for royals and royal events, *The Imperial March* for, composed for the Diamond Jubilee year of Queen Victoria, remains one of the most enduring.

The tenure of Sir Edward Elgar brought the relationship between music and royalty into the modern age, during which the activities of Master were generally exercised judiciously and rarely.

Sir Henry Walford Davies took over from Sir Edward Elgar after his death in 1934 and within a year of his appointment arranged a choral concert at The Albert

'Marriage of Albert Edward, Prince of Wales to Alexandra, Princess of Denmark' by Sir William Howard Russell (© The British Library)

Photographic portrait of Queen Victoria circa 1897 in commemoration of the Diamond Jubilee (© The British Library)

The 1953 coronation itself became a pivotal moment in British history since it was the first one to be televised (even if it was viewed mainly on minuscule monochrome TV receivers that were so rare in post-war Britain that groups of neighbours congregated in the homes of the fortunate few who owned a set).

It was this very fact, however, that contributed heavily to the public nature of the coronation and a subsequent revitalized public interest in royalty. For the first time ever, a large percentage of the population could actually see the spectacle and hear the music.

In fact, it was the music in general and *Zadok The Priest* in particular that provided the more authentic links with the past since the spectacle aspect of the proceedings was somewhat more contrived—organisers of the 'time-honoured' pageant were alleged to have consulted Herbert Wilcox's 1937 movie *Victoria The Great* for clues as to the types of carriages that might convincingly evoke a forgotten or non-existent processional tradition.

Hall to celebrate the King's Jubilee. He also participated in composing and arranging the coronation music for George VI, father of the future Queen Elizabeth II and a man reluctantly propelled to the throne by the abdication of his brother Edward who famously chose to marry a divorcée over being king (an assumed conflict of ambitions that did not deter the present Prince of Wales from taking a rather different course).

The coronation of Queen Elizabeth II in 1953 was celebrated by musical compositions from two Masters since it was a year in which the baton, so to speak, was being handed over. Sir Arnold Bax (Master from 1942-53) composed *The Coronation March* while the new incumbent Sir Arthur Bliss (Master from 1953-75) wrote a Processional.

Ralph Vaughan Williams, the distinguished composer who eschewed all formal honours except The Order of Merit in 1938, composed the motet *O Taste and See* for the coronation communion.

'Queen Elizabeth II in Coronation Robes' by Sir Norman Hartnell (The Royal Collection © 2005, Her Majesty Queen Elizabeth II)

For Elizabeth II's Silver Jubilee in 1977, Malcolm Williamson, one of the longest serving Masters (from 1975 to 2003) composed *Mass of Christ the King* and set to music a hymn written by the then Poet Laureate, Sir John Betjeman. Sir Peter Maxwell Davies took over as Master of the Queen's Music in March 2004.

Like everything else, the relationship between British royalty and the music that has served it down the centuries is changing. *Rule Britannia*, with its echoes of Empire, now seems to some people to go beyond benign traditionalism. *Jerusalem*, with its more tenuous connection to royalty seems eternally robust, while *Zadok The Priest* looks to have infinite mileage left.

In truth, over the years, royal music has often segued into patriotic anthem or religious affirmation, and its primary defining characteristics remain traditionalism and continuity.

All music, regardless of the art involved, has the capacity to stimulate a Proustian shiver that spontaneously evokes a time, a place or some memorable event in our lives.

For an institution as venerable as the British Royal family, celebratory music can achieve exactly the same thing, but on a far grander scale. In doing so, it directly links the familiar present to a past that predates not just ourselves but our ancestors too.

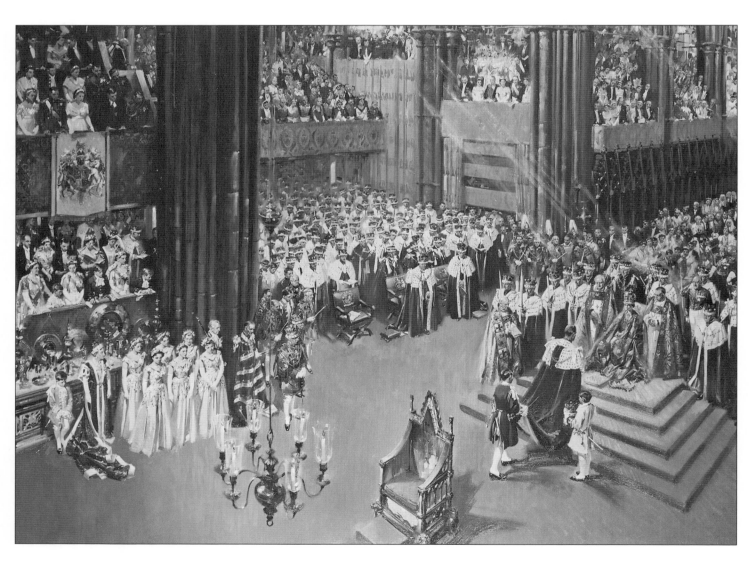

'The Coronation of Queen Elizabeth II, 2 June 1953' by Terence Cuneo (The Royal Collection © 2005, Her Majesty Queen Elizabeth II)

Part 1

Music For Royal Occasions

Imperial March
Composed by Sir Edward Elgar

Elgar composed the 'Imperial March' for Queen Victoria's Diamond Jubilee in 1897. In subsequent years, it was performed on several royal occasions, including the wedding of Princess Alice in 1904.

largamente

animato

allargando

Trumpet Voluntary
Composed by Jeremiah Clarke

Also known as 'The Prince of Denmark's March', this work has been performed at many royal events, including the wedding of Princess Mary (daughter of King George V) in 1922 and the Coronation of Elizabeth II in 1953.

Alla marcia

rall. al fine

Ped.   ✻

Zadok The Priest

Composed by George Frideric Handel

One of four anthems Handel composed for the Coronation of King George II in 1727,
'Zadok The Priest' has since been performed at every Coronation of the British Crown.

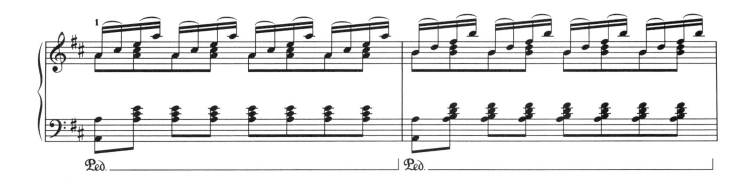

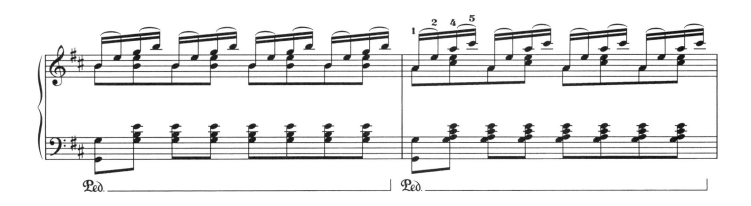

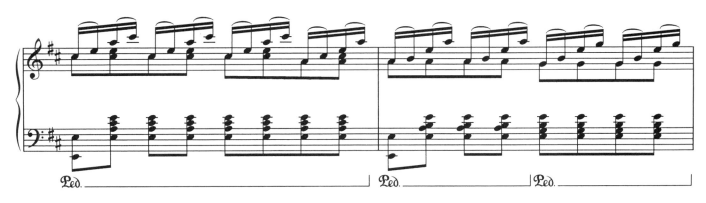

Allegro ($\quarternote$ = 128)

Menuets I and II
(from 'Music For The Royal Fireworks')
Composed by George Frideric Handel

Handel composed this music for King George II, to accompany festivities at
Green Park in celebration of the Treaty of Aix-la-Chapelle in 1749.

I Was Glad

Composed by Hubert Parry
Arranged by Derek Jones

This glorious anthem was composed in 1902 for the Coronation of King Edward VII. It has since been performed at every Coronation ceremony to mark the arrival of the monarch.

I was glad, glad when they said un - to me,

we will go,_____ we will go in-to the house of the

Lord. Our feet shall

stand in thy gates,_____ O Je - ru - sa - lem,_____ our feet shall

stand,_____ shall stand in thy gates,_____ our feet shall

rit.

stand,_____ shall stand in thy gates, O Je - ru - sa -

a tempo

- lem.

ff

mf

Je - ru -

- sa - lem_____ is build - - ed

as a ci - - ty, that is at

32

Vi - vat! Vi - vat! Vi - vat! Vi - vat!

ff

allargando

piú lento

slower

p

dim.

O pray for the peace of Je -

ru - sa - lem, _____ they shall pros - per that love _____ thee,

pray for the peace _____ of Je - ru - - - sa -

rit.

alla marcia

- lem, they shall pros - per that love _____ Thee

mf

Peace, _____ peace _____

O Taste And See

Composed by Ralph Vaughan Williams

Arranged by Derek Jones

This motet, originally for voices and organ, was composed especially for the
communion service at the Coronation of Elizabeth II in 1953.

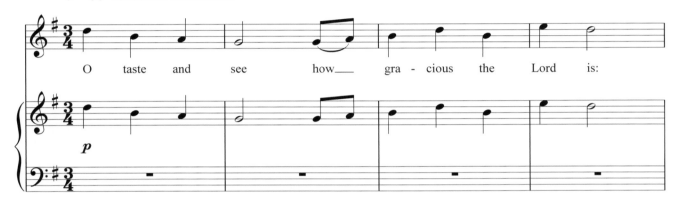

O taste and see how gra-cious the Lord is:

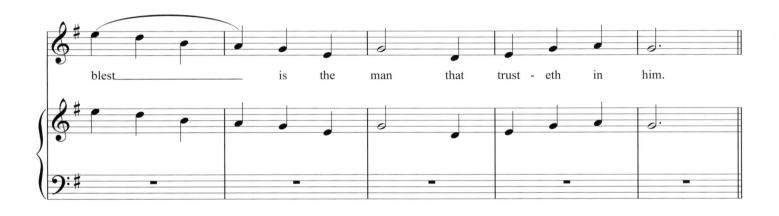

blest is the man that trust-eth in him.

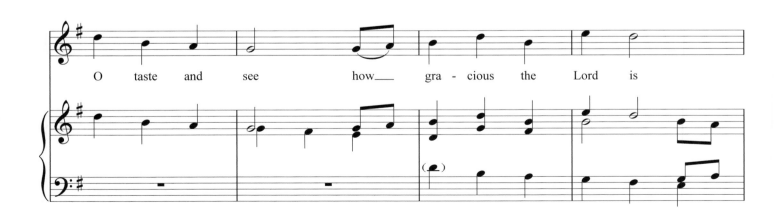

O taste and see how gra-cious the Lord is

blest_____ is the man that trust - eth in him._____ (Blest_____ is the man that trust - eth in him.) Blest_____ is the man_____ that_____ trust - eth in

L.H.

rit.

him, the man_____ that trust - eth_____ in him.

dim.

Rondo in D Minor
(from 'Abdelazer')
Composed by Henry Purcell

'Abdelazer' contains some of Purcell's finest orchestral music. This Rondo has been performed at many royal events, including the wedding of Charles and Diana in 1981.

Thou Wilt Keep Him In Perfect Peace

Composed by Samuel Sebastian Wesley

Arranged by Derek Jones

Composed especially for the Coronation of Elizabeth II, this sacred anthem by Samuel Wesley
accompanied the Homage portion of the ceremony.

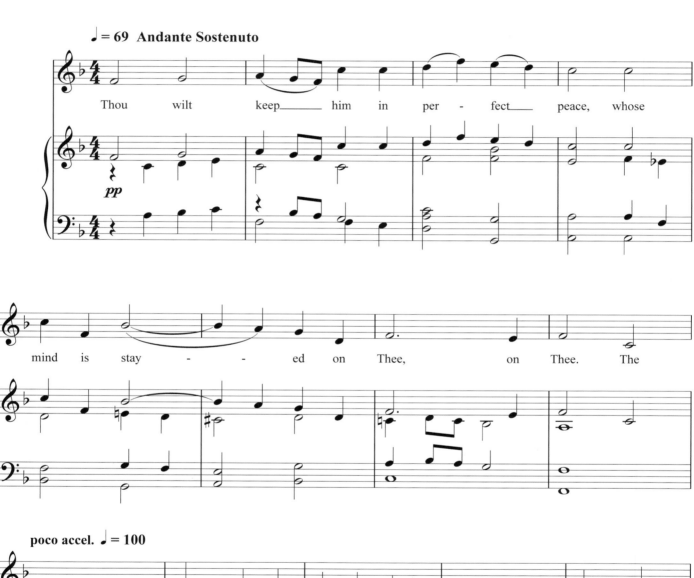

night is as clear as the day. The dark - ness and the

light to Thee, to Thee___ are___ both a -

Tempo I

- like,___ to___ Thee___ are both a - like.

God is light, and in Him is no___ dark - ness,___

in Him_____ is no____ dark-ness at all. O let my soul

live. O let my soul live, and it shall praise

poco accel. ♩ = 80

Thee, for Thine, Thine____ is the king - dom, the pow - er and the

mf

Glo - ry, for Thine____ is the king - dom, the pow - er and the

cresc.

44

glo - ry,_____ for ev - - - - er -

Tempo I

- more. Thou wilt keep_____ him in per - fect_____

peace, whose mind is stay - - ed on Thee, on

rit.

Thee, is stay - - ed on Thee.

Hornpipe
Composed by George Frideric Handel

This Hornpipe comes from Handel's famous 'Water Music,' composed in 1717
for a pleasure trip down the Thames by King George I and a gathering of English nobility.

Alla hornpipe

D.C. al Fine

PART II

TRADITIONAL FAVOURITES

I Vow To Thee My Country

Words by Cecil Spring Rice

Music by Gustav Holst

Cecil Spring Rice wrote the words for this patriotic song in 1918, and they were
set to the music of 'Jupiter' from Holst's 'The Planets' in 1921.

vow to thee, my coun - try, all earth - ly things a - bove, en -
- tire and whole and per - fect, the ser - vice of my love. The___
love that asks the ques - tions, the___ love that stands the test, that___
lays up - on the al - tar, the dear - est and the best. The___

love that nev - er fal - ters, the love that pays the price, the____

love that makes un - daunt - ed, the fi - nal sac - ri - fice. The____

love that asks the ques - tions, the____ love that stands the test, that____

lays up - on the al - tar, the dear - est and the best. The____

love that nev - er fal - ters, the love that pays the price, the ___

love that makes un - daunt - ed, the fi - nal sac - ri -

- fice.

2. And ___ peace.

Verse 2:
And there's another country, I've heard of long ago
Most dear to them that love her, most great to them that know
We may not count her armies, we may not see her King
Her fortress is a faithful heart, her pride is suffering
And soul by soul and silently her shining bounds increase
And her ways are ways of gentleness and all her paths are peace.

Greensleeves
Traditional

The true origins of this folk tune are uncertain, but many believe that it was written
by Henry VIII, who was an amateur performer and composer.

Andante cantabile

Land Of Hope And Glory
(Pomp And Circumstance March No.1)
Words by Arthur Benson & Music by Sir Edward Elgar

Elgar's Pomp and Circumstance March No.1 became the tune to 'Land of Hope and Glory',
a patriotic anthem evoking the glory of the British Empire.

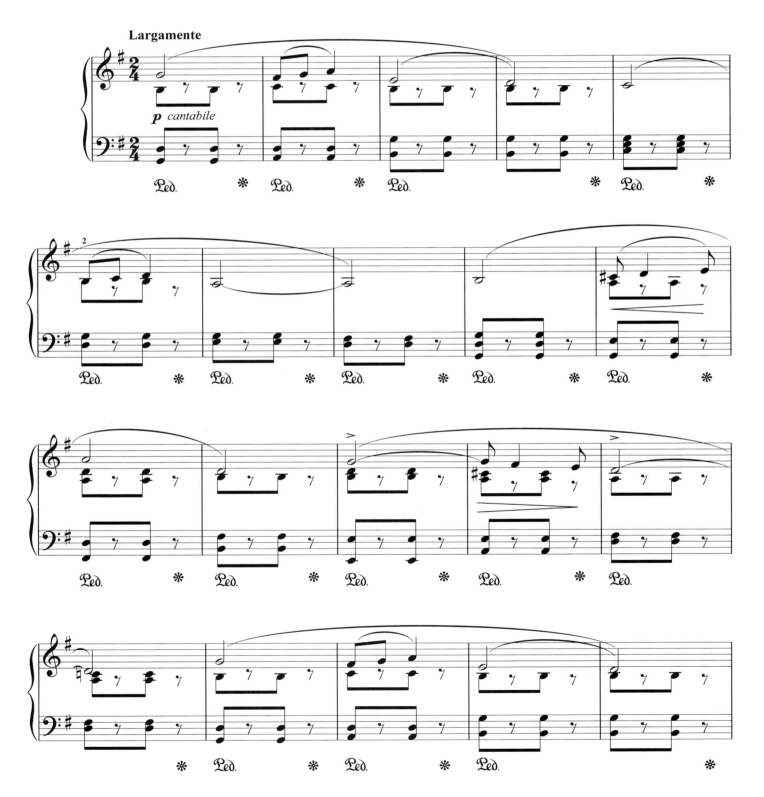

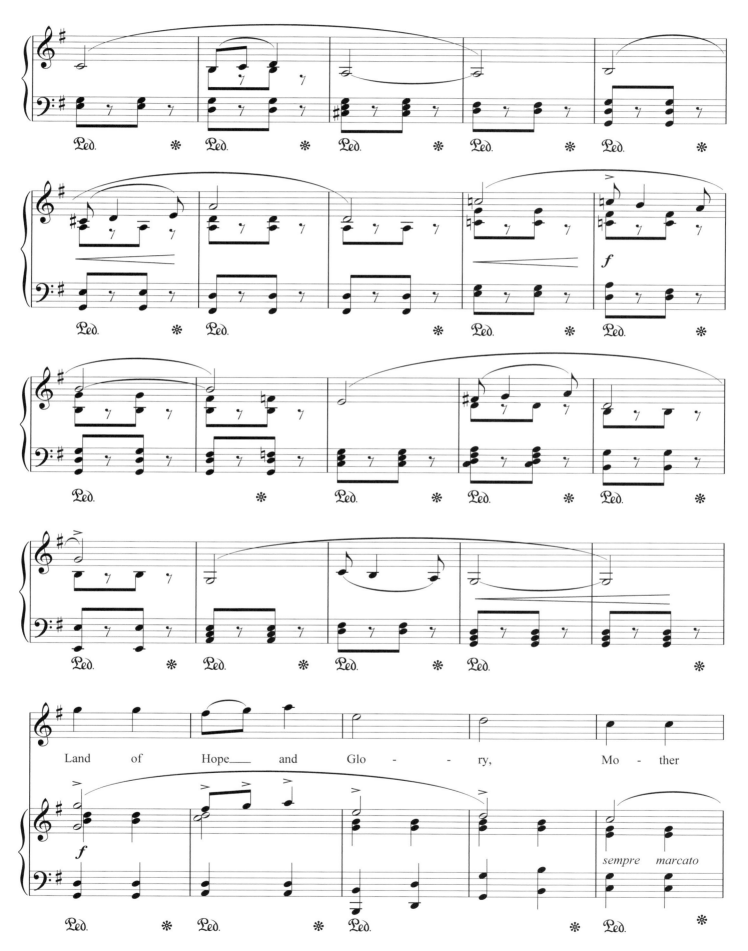

Land of Hope__ and Glo - ry, Mo - ther

57

God, who made thee might - - y,

make thee might - ier yet.

God, who made thee might - - y,

make thee might - ier yet.

There'll Always Be An England

Words & Music by Ross Parker & Hughie Charles

Written in 1939, this patriotic English song became popular
during World War II, as sung by Vera Lynn.

I give you a toast, la-dies and gen-tle-men, I give you a toast, la-dies and gen-tle-men, "May this fair land we

love so well in dig - ni - ty and free - dom dwell" Tho'

colla voce　　　　　　　　　　　　　　　　　　　　　　　**a tempo**

worlds may change and go aw - ry, while there is still one voice to cry.

There'll al - ways be an Eng - land while

there's a coun - try lane,　wher - ev - er there's a cot - tage small be -

Ped.

61

side a field of grain. There'll al - ways be an Eng - land while

there's a bu - sy street; wher - ev - er there's a turn - ing wheel a

mil - lion march - ing feet. Red, white and blue, what does it

mean to you? Sure - ly you're proud, shout it a - loud, Brit - ons a - wake, the

Em - pire too, we can de - pend on you, free - dom re -
-mains these are the chains, noth - ing can break,_____ there'll al - ways be an
Eng - land and Eng - land shall be free, if
Eng - land means as much to you as Eng - land means to

me. There'll al - ways be an Eng - land while

there's a coun - try lane; wher - ev - er there's a

cot - tage small be - side a field of grain. There'll

al - ways be an Eng - land while there's a bu - sy

mains these are the chains, noth - ing can break,_____ there'll al - ways be an

Eng - land and Eng - land shall be free,_____ if

Eng - land means as much to you as Eng - land means_____

to me._____

Rule Britannia

Composed by Thomas Arne

Originally written as part of Thomas Arne's masque 'Alfred', 'Rule Britannia'
has become an integral part of the Last Night of the Proms.

a - zure main, a - rose, a - rose, a - rose from out the a - zure main.

This was the char - ter, the char - ter of the land, and

guar - dian an - gels sung this strain: Rule Bri - tan - nia! Bri-

-tan - nia rule the waves. Bri - tons nev - er, nev - er, nev - er shall be slaves. 2. The

Verse 2:
The nations, not so blest as thee
Must in their turn, to tyrants fall
Must in their turn, must in their turn, to tyrants fall
While thou shalt flourish, shalt flourish great and free
The dread and envy of them all.

Rule Britannia! *etc.*

Verse 3:
Still more majestic shalt thou rise
More dreadful, from each foreign stroke
More dreadful, more dreadful from each foreign stroke
As the loud blast that tears the skies
Serves but to root thy native oak.

Rule Britannia! *etc.*

Verse 4:
Thee haughty tyrants ne'er shall tame
All their attempts to bend thee down
All their attempts, all their attempts to bend thee down
Will but arouse thy generous flame
But work their woe and thy renown.

Rule Britannia! *etc.*

Verse 5:
To thee belongs the rural reign
Thy cities shall with commerce shine
Thy cities shall, thy cities shall with commerce shine
All thine shall be the subject main
And every shore it circles thine.

Rule Britannia! *etc.*

Verse 6:
The Muses, still with freedom found
Shall to thy happy coast repair
Shall to thy happy coast, thy happy coast repair
Blest isle! With matchless beauty crowned
And manly hearts to guard the fair.

Rule Britannia! *etc.*

Jerusalem

Composed by Hubert Parry

The work for which Sir Hubert Parry is best remembered, 'Jerusalem'
remains one of the nation's most beloved anthems.

-sire! Bring me my spear, oh, clouds un - fold! Bring me my cha - ri - ot of

fire! I will not cease from men - tal fight, nor shall my sword sleep in my

hand. 'Till we have built Je - ru - sa - lem in Eng - land's

green and plea - sant land.

PART III

PATRIOTIC TRIBUTES

Queen Elizabeth Her Galliard

Composed by John Dowland

A 'galliard' is a dance that was popular in the courts of the 16th and 17th centuries. Dowland wrote this stately galliard as a tribute to Queen Elizabeth I.

Moderato (♩ = 84)

poco rall.

Thou Knowest, Lord

Composed by Henry Purcell

This work, one in a vast collection of music Purcell composed for royal figures,
was written for Queen Mary II's funeral in 1695.

Slow

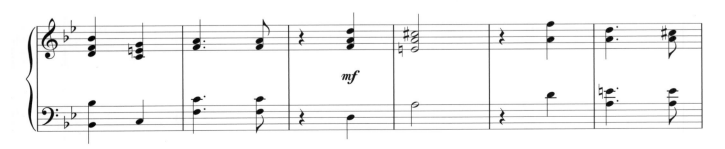

In A Golden Coach (There's A Heart Of Gold)

Words & Music by Ronald Jamieson

This popular song was written as a tribute to Elizabeth II
on the occasion of her Coronation in 1953.

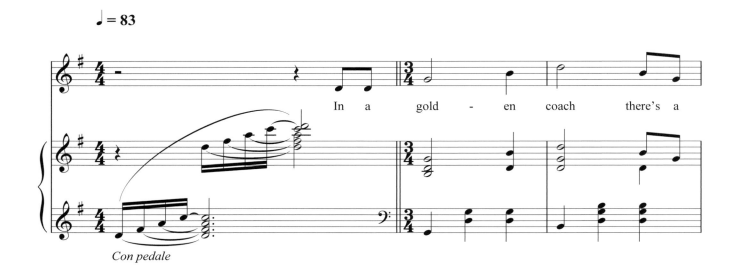

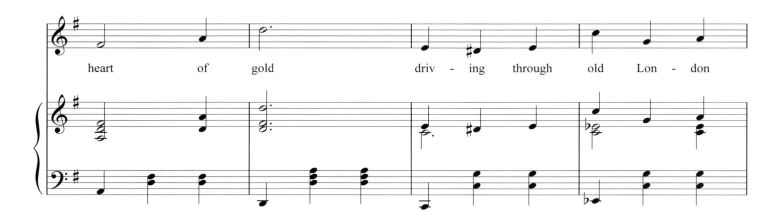

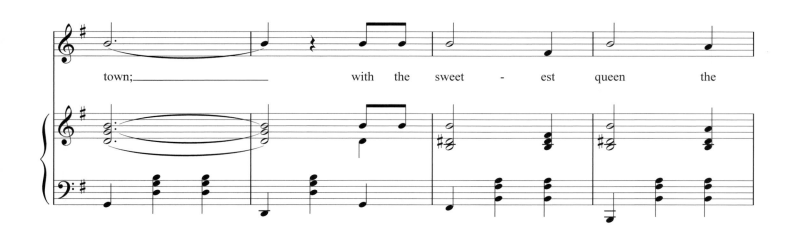

world's   ev - er   seen,   wear - ing   her
gold - - en   crown._____   As   she
drives   in   state   through   the   pal - - ace
gate,   her   beau - ty   the   whole   world   will

see._____ In a gold - en coach there's a

To Coda ⊕

heart of gold that be - longs to you and

me._____

As she gold that be - longs to you and me.

God Bless The Prince Of Wales

Words by John Ceiriog Hughes & Music by Henry Brinley Richards

This song was written in 1863 to celebrate the twenty-first birthday of the future
King Edward VII, and his upcoming marriage to Alexandra of Denmark.

Maestoso

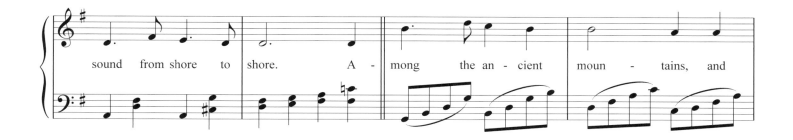

sound from shore to shore. A - mong the an - cient moun - tains, and

from our love - ly vales, oh let the pray'r re -

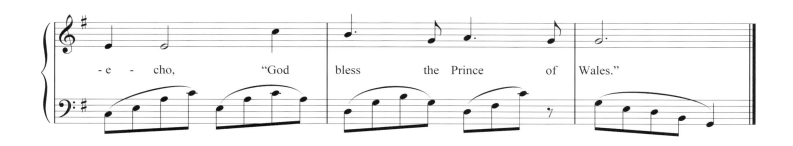

- e - cho, "God bless the Prince of Wales."

Verse 2:
Should hostile bands or danger
Ere threaten our fair isle
May God's strong arm protect us
May Heav'n still on us smile
Above the throne of England
May fortune's star long shine!
And round its sacred bulwarks
The olive branches twine.

Among the ancient mountains
And from our lovely vales
Oh let the pray'r re-echo
"God bless the Prince of Wales."

Here's A Health Unto Her Majesty

Traditional

The origins of this song are uncertain, but it was likely intended not for a Queen, but a King—many believe that it was written to celebrate the Coronation of Charles II as King of Scotland in 1650.

British Grenadiers

Traditional

One of the most familiar regimental marches, 'British Grenadiers'
was sung on the battlefield as early as 1777.

In march time

2. Those heroes of antiquity ne'er saw a cannon-ball,
    Or knew the force of powder to slay their foes withal;
    But our brave boys do know it, and banish all their fears;
    Sing tow, row, row, sing tow, row, row, for the British Grenadiers.

3. Whene'er we are commanded to storm the palisades
    Our leaders march with fusees, and we with hand-grenades;
    We throw them from the glacis, about the enemies' ears;
    Sing tow, row, row, sing tow, row, row, for the British Grenadiers.

4. And when the siege is over, we to the town repair
    The townsmen cry, "Hurrah, boys! here comes a Grenadier
    Here come the Grenadiers, my boys, who know no doubts or fears!"
    Sing tow, row, row, sing tow, row, row, for the British Grenadiers.

5. Then let us fill a bumper and drink a health to those
    Who carry caps and pouches, and wear the loupéd clothes;
    May they and their commanders live happy all their years
    Sing tow, row, row, sing tow, row, row, for the British Grenadiers.

The National Anthem

Traditional

happy and glorious, long to____ reign____ ov - er us; God____ save the Queen!

poco rit.

marc.

a tempo

Thy choic - est gifts in store on Her be

pleased to pour; long may She reign!

May She de - fend our laws, and ev - er give us cause

to sing___ with___ heart and voice: God___ save the

rit.

Queen! God save the Queen!